Inside Out Woman

THE COLLECTED POETRY OF
DORIS M. ROSS
(1927-1986)

Phillip A. Ross, Editor

Marietta, Ohio

ISBN: 978-0-9839046-9-4
Edition: 12.1.2014

Published by

Pilgrim Platform
149 E. Spring St.,
Marietta, Ohio, 45750
www.pilgrim-platform.org

Special thanks to David C. Ross for scanning and digitizing
the photos.

Printed in the United States of America

*For
Family & Friends*

BOOKS BY PHILLIP A. ROSS

The Work At Zion—A Reckoning, Two-volume set, 772 pages, 1996.

Practically Christian—Applying James Today, 135 pages, 2006.

The Wisdom of Jesus Christ in the Book of Proverbs, 414 pages, 2006.

Marking God's Word—Understanding Jesus, 324 pages, 2006.

Acts of Faith—Kingdom Advancement, 326 pages, 2007.

Informal Christianity—Refining Christ's Church, 136 pages, 2007.

Engagement—Establishing Relationship in Christ, 104 pages, 1996, 2008.

It's About Time! — The Time Is Now, 40 pages. 2008.

The Big Ten—A Study of the Ten Commandments, 105 pages, 2001, 2008.

Arsy Varsy—Reclaiming The Gospel in First Corinthians, 406 pages, 2008.

Varsy Arsy—Proclaiming The Gospel in Second Corinthians, 356 pages, 2009.

Colossians—Christos Singularis, 278 pages, 2010.

Rock Mountain Creed—The Sermon on the Mount, 310 pages, 2011.

The True Mystery of the Mystical Presence, 355 pages, 2011.

Peter's Vision of Christ's Purpose in First Peter, 340 pages, 2011.

Peter's Vision of The End in Second Peter, 184 pages, 2012.

The Religious History of Nineteenth Century Marietta, Thomas Jefferson Summers, 124 pages, 1903, 2012 (editor).

Conflict of Ages—The Great Debate of the Moral Relations of God and Man, Edward Beecher, 489 pages, 1853, 2012 (editor).

Concord Of Ages—The Individual And Organic Harmony Of God And Man, Edward Beecher, D. D., Phillip A. Ross, Editor, 524 pages, 2013.

Ephesians—Recovering the Vision of a Sustainable Church in Christ, 417 pages, 2013.

Poet Tree—Root, Branch & Sap, 72 pages, 2013.

I am standing upon the seashore. A ship at my side spreads her white sails to the morning breeze and starts for the blue ocean …. I stand and watch her, until at length she hangs like a speck in a white cloud that has come down to mingle with others. Then someone at my side says, "There, she's gone!"

Gone where? Gone from my sight, that is all. She is just as large in mast and hull and spar as she was when she left my side ….

Her diminished size is in me—not in her! And just at the moment when someone at my side says, "There, she's gone," there are other eyes watching her coming, and other voices ready to take up the glad shout, "There she comes!"

—Anonymous

TABLE OF CONTENTS

INTRODUCTION

To introduce one's mother is necessarily a subjective and emotional process, and it should be. Mothers are always involved in our experience of love. To a significant extent mothers shape our earliest experience of love. My task here is made more difficult because as I write this, Doris lies on her death bed; at 59 years old she contracted brain cancer. My relationship with my mother has undergone several processes of change—all of them good, all of them enriching my understanding of her as a person. I offer my words here that your appreciation of her work may be increased.

Doris always intended to publish this volume of poetry. No one ever imagined that she would be denied the completion of that process herself. I, then, have taken it upon myself to tidy up her working manuscript and finish her project. I have endeavored to leave her work as I found it, making only small corrections here and there.

I have some questions about the dates that are attached to many of her poems. I do not believe that the dates assigned by her to many of these poems indicate the date that she wrote a particular piece, but rather indicate the date that she last edited a particular poem. When we see several poems with the same date, then, we can understand that to be a period of deep reflection when she reworked some of her poetry.

I have worked from a nearly complete manuscript and have corrected punctuation and capitalization here and there—as I expect she would have done, and have added titles to some of her untitled poem, indicated with the titles in parentheses. Other editing was done as she indicated in her own hand.

Special thanks to my brother, David, for supplying digitized photos, and to my wife, Stephanie, for her careful attention to detail and patience with my muse.

In Doris' poetry you will catch a glimpse of her deepest struggles and joys. You will have an opportunity to see a side of her that you may not know. She was by her own admission a "strong, silent, sufferer." It was not part of her constitution to complain, and at times she even chose to withhold her feelings. If you know her history—her story—your appreciation of her poetry will be deeper. Much of her personal life is reflected in the pages that follow.

Doris was both a mother and a career woman. Her first marriage ended in divorce (and a child—me) within its first year. She remarried several years later and raised five children. Her brood acquainted her with all the highs and lows of motherhood. She returned to work when her youngest children were in high school.

Her working career was marked with a series of rapid promotions. Beginning as a secretary, she climbed the ladder of success in the field of her deepest interest and concern: education. Though her own formal education ended after only one year of college, she was self-educated through her voracious reading habit. Some say that she read in order to maintain sanity as she

raised her brood. She soon became an Administrative
Editor with The Education Commission Of The States
(ECS) in Denver, Colorado, a position that usually
required a Master's Degree. Doris had a brilliant mind
and was fortunate enough to be in a position in which
her talents were recognized by her employer. Doris'
poetry attests to the fact that intellectual acumen and
emotional sensitivity often go hand in hand.

The cross that she bore, as you will see in her
poetry, was ultimately staked in the soil of her emo-
tional life, or more precisely, her love live. Her second
marriage ended in divorce after some twenty-five years.
Yet because of children and circumstance that relation-
ship was never completely severed. In the pages that
follow you will come to understand a little of her
sensitivity and emotional struggles with her self, her job,
and her love.

You will also note a decidedly religious flavor in
much of her poetry. Doris was a committed Christian
and a dedicated church woman. Yet her faith was not
blind, but rather was won through her struggles with
this life and its injustices, both personally and socially.
Her's was a faith that had made friends with doubt, and
her doubt served to sharpen the intellectual edge of her
faith.

Doris was a person who was fully engaged in being
a person. Always active in her community and church,
she also went on in her work to "hobnob" with intel-
lectuals and politicians, networking with such unlikely
yokefellows. She had a way of assisting people to
express themselves more fully and more clearly, whether
she was working with them as an editor or relating with
them just as a friend, in conversation as well as in print.

She would not allow anyone to put her on any kind

of pedestal. She always maintained with the utmost integrity that she was an ordinary person. She sought no special accolades, though to her public dissatisfaction (but I think to her private satisfaction) she received some awards and recognition through her work and through her church.

When she began to write poetry in earnest hope of publishing, she adopted the pen name, "dross." In her papers I found a copy of the hymn, "How Firm A Foundation," with the last stanzas of the fourth verse underlined. It reads,

Thy dross to consume, and thy gold to refine;
Thy dross to consume, and thy gold to refine.

Dross is, according to Webster, "waste or foreign matter." She liked the name. It kept her humble

But one of her associates at ECS felt differently about her new name. He thought it was unnecessarily unflattering. He writes:

Dross

dross?   No way.
Abbreviations, acronyms, logos—all are
        useful and understandable
            but not if,
                in their final form,
                    they present a meaning that is
                        inaccurate
                            unflattering or
                                unacceptable.

dross?   Not so.
Not for a colleague
    who sparkles with life
        meets adversity with courage
            who is gracious to all
                writes with consummate skill
                    and passion;
                        learns and
                            knows and
                                can tell.
dross?   Not for me.
Gold is where you find it
    Not just the hard metal from earth
        But in people, exemplified in those qualities
        of ability
                compassion
                humor
                    judgment and
                        belief
That allow men and women to
    work together
        to respect each other
            to accomplish much
                and enjoy each day
                    as it comes.
dross?   Let it end.
Doris will do. And all
    will know
        whom is meant and
            what she represents!

                                    —Warren G. Hill

    I cannot bracket my own subjectivity as I try to
evaluate her poetry. But in my best judgment, I believe

that her work is genuinely good. Her love of language and appreciation for its economical and creative use result in a style that is at once eloquent, yet unencumbered, even wisely innocent. As she bears her soul, note how both her sense of humor and the acuteness of her sensitivity—her pain, play against one another. I commend it to you for your enjoyment and edification

Phillip A. Ross
July 1986
St. Louis, Missouri

October 2014
Marietta, Ohio

Collected Poetry

HAPPINESS

Happiness—what is this thing?
Is it something that men can bring?
Or is it something just for the heart
To cherish until it will stay, or depart?

Is happiness a mental state?
A thing of science, or does it relate
To the Spirit? Is perfection of soul
Needed for this, the whole world's goal?

Happiness—what is this thing?
Something to make all humanity sing?
Who knows what it is? Who can define
Happiness is a word or a line?

It must be ecstasy—a bliss to desire
Something to seek with all of the fire
Of a neglected self. My God will define
Happiness when he makes it mine.

1945

Free Gift Wrapping

Time:
>   —the measured package in which the gift of life
>   arrives;
>   —discarded, carelessly spent, penuriously hoarded;
>   —thoughtfully given, callously received;
>   —bought and sold for a pittance;
>   —shepherded;
>   —priceless.

Time:
>   —to be without it is to render ability useless;
>   —to use it unwisely is to avoid living's essence.

Time:
>   —to sell it all is to reject love;
>   —to give it all is impractically admirable;
>   —to keep it all is selfish heresy;
>   —precious.

Time:
>   —divided, spent;
>   —bought, sold;
>   —given, taken;
>   —wasted, used.

Time:
>   God's exclusive gift wrapper;
>   Limit One.

1964

New, Father

Stop, world!
I have a miracle here.
He wants to get on.

Look, world!
I am filled with him.
He is beautifully unsurpassed.

Listen, world!
God has given me a son.
Unique, fabulous!

Flesh of my flesh
Bone of my bone
Bearer of my name.

Accept him, world!
Love him, nurture him.
Help him grow.

This miracle of mine
Is not mine.
He is yours.

1964

Bus Ride

Tired.
She's weary of struggle.
Her hair, bleached, stringy
(Once a fluffy gold)
Obscures her face
As, tenderly,
She guides her blue-eyed cherub
To a seat.

Slumped.
Her shabby blue-jeaned legs
Sprawled. Her arm,
Protective, around the child.
A ride
Over the path
Of poverty.

                                            1964

Lost

Imprisoned by your youth
You rattle the bars fiercely
Move your cage
To another locale.

Huddled with others
You conform in your departure
From life's exposure.
You seek something in nothingness.

Deliberately lost
You flutter, finding complexity
In simplicity.
You grasp fruitlessly
For new rules.

Pitiable one! Foetal sage!
Unknowingly, you push at time,
Blinded by your disorder
You cannot see
Your cure.

1964

NINE TO FIVE

Buzz, chatter, yak.
Sip, munch, mince.
Tailored color
Tasteful jewels
The cocktail party.

Veiled dislike
Covered contempt
Shuttered boredom
Smile. It's
The Happy Hour.

1964

Hot Coals And Bare Feet

One—
Barefoot,
Exposed, vulnerable.
His invisible cloak of faith
Carries him ever forward.

His pain, masked with purpose
His joy enhanced by openness
Clothed in nakedness
He lives.

Two—
Encumbered by
Overt impedimentia
Fingering his security
He lingers—

Fearfully contemplating
The hot coals of life.
Armored, unimpregnable,
He dies.

1964

No Thank You, Please

Why do you thank me?
I did for you
To please myself.
Acknowledgment
Was not my aim.

I love me.
I live with me.
Leave me be
And let me help.

The Zoo

Boarding Tour Bus 12
For the Bowery
Eager, expectant faces, anticipating
Filth, despair, poverty
—Revolution. A thrill?

Countenance curiously unalive
Framed in aluminum and glass
Protected from the rankness
Outside.

A wrinkled, shuffling hag
Nudges her companion
Points, stares,
Look!

Who's caged?

(AMBIGUITY)

The only difference between a
woman's ambiguity and a man's
is her man-given freedom to
express hers.

A powerful intellect in a man
is much admired; the same thing
in a woman is greatly feared.

1964

Pussycat

Pussycat, pussycat,
Where have you been?
Writing a book?
That's nice.

Pussycat, pussycat,
I want you now
Stop talking politics
Sweety-pie.

Pussycat, pussycat,
I'd like to play
Painting a picture?
How cute.

Pussycat, pussycat,
Where have you gone?
Pussycat?
Pussycat?

1964

Forty

Incredible!
It just can't be.
What have I done.
For eternity?

Worked a little
Played much more
But what have I done
To jack up my score?

Lots of children
Housework and stuff
O, God, My God!
It isn't enough.

Where is the book
I was going to write?
Where is the fame?
Out of sight, overnight!

Tomorrow I'll start
The projects I planned
My time must have slipped
Out of mind, out of hand.

1966

Order

I cry for order!
Let all around me
Be tidy, arranged,
Neat. I slave
To get it clean.

A slattern, I
Have not the time
To dust
The disordered recess
Of my mind.

1966

NOW AND THEN

Here is my place.
I must sit in it.
Why do I strain,
Yearning for horizons
Beyond?

Here is my job.
I must do it.
And in the doing,
Will my horizons come,
Unbidden, to me?

1968

All Is God Is Love

Love accepts me
For what I am;
It goes further to
Appreciate me for this.
Love sees what
I can become;
It goes further to
Help me toward this vision.
Love asks nothing of me;
Expects a great deal,
But is not disappointed
When I fall short.
Instead it offers me
Hope and courage
When whether I realize it
Or not, I need it the most.

This accepting love is there
At my blackest moments;
It is also present,
Rejoicing with me,
When by some mischance
Good fortune,
Or through my own effort,
 I triumph.

Love accepts me
When I am most unlovable;
When I behave badly;
When I fail to
Consider those who

Depend on me;
When I am so self-oriented
That I not only do not
Function well,
But ignore the needs
Of others.

Love needs me, too,
And lets me know that need.
But when I cannot respond,
Love waits patiently and
Perhaps eternally
With me.

Love finds something in me
That is beautiful
And helps it to grow.
Love helps me to recognize
And obliterate
Those parts of me
That are ugly.

Love disciplines me.
It helps me to
Accept my imperfections
While being aware of them.
It does not make me perfect,
But when love is present,
I strive to be better.

Love comforts me
When I am sad,
But it does not allow me
The luxury of self-pity.

Love diminishes my desire
For self-indulgence;
It mysteriously impels me
To offer myself
To others.
It does not permit
My self-glorification
Because it is so much larger
Than I.

Love is not innocent;
It is wise beyond belief.
It uses its wisdom
To keep me
From self-deception
And apathy. It will not
Let me hate; it will
Help me to understand.
It is exclusive to me
Because of my individuality;
It is inclusive for all
Because of our commonality.

Love makes me
Aware of my life.
And finding it precious,
More aware of the preciousness
Of the life around me.
Love makes me love,
Not only in return,
But with an intensity,
With which ease
Is amplified many times over.

I have much to learn
About love;
Its nuances, its oneness,
Its wholeness.
Perhaps someday I will live
Close enough to love
To say with truth, humility,
And a measure of approval
From my Creator,
"Not only am I loved,
But I do love."

1972

*Published in the Journal Of Current Social Issues,
Vol 14., No. 2, Spring 1977, Division of Higher
Education, United Church Board for Homeland
Ministries.*

I Am

Thank you, Lord.
I have stopped asking
"Who am I?"
Nor do I worry
About who I was
Or who I will be.
The "I" of yesterday
And of tomorrow
Are not the same,
Nor are they
The "me" of today.
My old question
"Why are you here?"
Puzzles me no more.
I am, quite simply, here.

Thank you, Lord.
You created me unique;
Gifted me abundantly
With will, intelligence,
Creativity, sensitivity.
Your purpose evolves
Unplanned by me.
I am. I am here.
I am here now.
I think. I feel. I do.
I grow. I love.
My significance
Is eternally within You.

Thank you, Lord.

It is more than enough.
On me has Your light shined.
I am! I am!

Published in the Journal Of Current Social Issues, Vol 14., No. 2, Spring 1977, Division of Higher Education, United Church Board for Homeland Ministries.

To My Child

I love you.
Feed yourself.
Stand up!
  (Do not deign
   to see my
   outstretched hand.)

I love you.
Make your own mistakes.
Cry alone.
  (Know, but be not
   aware of my
   sobs.)

I love you.
Earn your own reward.
Rejoice in solitude.
  (See, but do not
   notice my
   preening pride.)

I love you.
Get away from me.
Be strong.
  (Feel not
   my pain
   when you leave.)

I love you.
Please
Love me back.
  (God give me
   strength to
   let you go.)

1974

To Style Or Not To Style

a comma here a cap right there
but next time round no dice
to edit my material
one must know how to splice

i try to do it right you know
i really write quite well
but when I face a printing press
i suddenly cant spel

do commas come before an and
or not and tell me please
why can't i split a word today
with flair elan and ease

dont tell me to return to school
I read a lot and know
that write is right and wrong is left
where do the footnotes go
alas alack a swinger I
each day confront catastrophe
while dashing wild and free through verbs
I space out the apostrophe

                                        1974

Hope

Hope   lost will be found
Hope   fettered is not bound
Hope   present is not sought
Hope   absent fear will wrought
Hope   distant will come near
Hope   helpless God will hear
Hope   help will be faith
Hope   dropped is sorrow's wraith
Hope   abandoned does not die
Hope   nourished will stay nigh
Hope   basic grips us all
Hope   total hears God's call.

WAITING

I am always here
Waiting.
With a scorched and
Wilted meal
With clean sheets
And polished nails.
Perfumed, impatient.

Ready to welcome
With a smile
And a kiss.
Almost always.
I live with anxiety
Mistrust and hope.
Despair.

Once I believed.
Now I know
Where he is, but
Not what he does.
I can imagine.
And I do.
Many things.

I wait for him
Always here.
I cry for him.
Waiting here.
Now and then
I am angry, resentful

While he fills another life
Mine empties.

Soon, perhaps
I will grow weary
Of waiting.
I will abandon
Hope; embrace suspicion.
I will not wait.
Not here.
Not for him.

Fool

You fool! Why do you
Sit here waiting for him?
When you could be out
Having a lovely affair?

What about John or Frank
Or Charles or William?
Surely one appeals
To you—take a dare!

Another psyche could be
Your panacea, fool.
Another body might be
New heights for you.

You timid, vacillating
Simpleton! You
Waste your life, and
Worse, your love.

You fool! You listen not
To good advice.
You are condemned
By hope to wait forever.

Coward

I am a coward.
I have not the guts to leave.
Where would I go?
I have no one
I will trust.
My children—
Do not need me. They
Seek their own lives.
My man does not
Find me worthy
Of his time.

I do not wish
To burden my friends.
Or strangers.
Or God.

I must go.
Where-to-whom-when?
I am unnecessary
To my man.
And I am
A coward without him.
He is not here ....

I Remember

A woman now
I remember.
My birthing times.
The first, too soon,
Unwanted, terrifying
Unplanned product
Of a broken relationship.
Pink-plump-helpless-lovable.
Ready to love.
The second (two it was)
Joyful pain
Which did not hurt.
Sensual, throbbing, erotic, fierce.
Dramatic; commonplace.
Triumphant
Shivering.
Two more to hold
With my heart.
The last.
A swift arrival
Again unplanned but
Eagerly anticipated.
One who earned
Without trying, my love
By being.
I remember.
I am
A woman now.

Incommunicado

A woman, I
remember now
Our wedding year.
I remember the time
I began to
Dance and sing
On a darkened street
Till you shushed me
"You'll wake people up."
So I resumed
The dignity befitting
A married lady.
Because I love you
And wanted to be
All
You wanted me to be.
I put my joy
Inside of me.

A woman, I
remember now
I called you
"My beloved."
You brushed it off
Impatiently.
"Don't be silly."
And so
I put my foolish sentiment
Safely inside me.
I wanted to be

All
You wanted me to be.

A woman then
I remember now
My homemade clothes
My unset hair
And your admiring glances
At other girls
Better endowed.
I buried my envy
Deep within.
I could not be
What you admired.

A woman always
I remember
Your casual words
"Many bodies, any body
Can sate a man's desire."
I looked at mine
Was it not
Given with love,
Better? No.
I pushed my own
Desire within
And made a game
Of love.
I wanted to be
What you wanted
Me to be.

A woman forever
I remember best

The times
(Oh, not enough!)
My prisoned moods
Escaped.
Soared. Ballooned.
Expanded. Overflowed.
Until I
Prompted by
Sudden remembrance
Caught them
And put them back
With stronger bonds.

A woman, I
Remember
The beginning of
Your change.
Bewildered, love,
I loved you still.
Confused. I did not
Understand
Your battering
Of my soul.
With joy,
Sentiment,
Love,
Openness
Unveiled at last to me
You asked me
To be me.
You wanted to love
My inside now.
I did not
See your love

Before.
Dear God!
A circle forms!
Who is me?
A woman again
Can I remember?

Pillow Talk

"Talk to me."
"Okay. What about?"
"Just talk."
"I need a subject."
"What's on your mind?"
"Nothing. Everything."
"Love me?"
"Of course."
"Then say it."
"No."
"Why?"
"Because you asked me."
"Why must I ask you?"
"You needn't. You know."
"I need to hear it."
"I know. But words—"
"Are meaningless."
"What is love?"
"I don't know."
"Define it."
"I can't—but—"
"What?"
"I love you."
"What?"
"I love you."
"I know."
"Talk to me."
"I love you too."

WHY

Why do I love you?
Damned if I know.
You turn me on.
And I love you.
I turn you on
And I love you more.
I see your sensitivity;
It sometimes
Looks like mood.
Your gaiety is catching;
Short-lived at times.
Your tenderness melts me;
Then unnerves me.
Your confidence comforts me;
Then shakes me.
Your tenacity amazes me;
Then runs out.
Your soul finds me;
Then escapes me.
Your strength encourages me;
Then defeats me.
Why do I love you?
Damned if I know.

Puzzle

You say you love me
Yet you see
her
every day.
I do not understand.

Perplexed, I ask
you why
You counter with
a question.
"Do I not see you
every day?"

"She needs me.
I must go."
(I need you too.
Please stay.)

You love her too
You do not comprehend
my distress.
"Possessive," you say.
"Selfish." I am.

"You have so much,"
You say. I nod.
"I have it all—
but you."

"Here I am."
You're fretful now
(And well you should
be. I ask
too much.)

My love is not
large enough
to share you.
I know. I try
to tolerate
your absences—
your constant thought
of her.

I do not always
succeed.

Why do you stay
with me? I
do not make you happy.

I demand too much
and give too little
—or perhaps
you do not see
my gifts.

Your love is too large
for me
to understand.
I wonder if it is not too large
for her
as well.

I cannot live with you
this way. I must.
For I cannot live without you
any way.

I love you.
But I don't know how
to understand.

BALLAD

I'll tell you a story of love that was lost
And found in great glory at unmeasured cost
The man that she married was straight and sure
Tender, demanding, his love for her
He worked very hard to make plenty of time
To love her and hold her in moments sublime.
He served his community, played with his kids
Thought of his business, had time for her bids.
The girl that he married was much the same
Until energy lapsed with her busy fame
While she kept a nice house and took care of her kids.
There never seemed time for her husband's bids.
She love him sincerely and he loved her back
But moments together they seemed to lack
The words "I love you, dear" were seldom exchanged.
As life's busy schedule made them feel estranged.

He found metamorphosis quite slowly, you know
Philosophy for this would come and would go
But finally finding a comfortable niche
He offered his wide love to all without hitch.
And suddenly, wonder of wonders, she knew
He was changed to a man of a different hue.
Her mold didn't fit him; its shape he outgrew
He found new relationships, more than a few
While puzzled and patient, she tired to pretend
That she didn't miss him for hours on end.
She needed him badly, but he didn't know
Her pride wouldn't tell him her life was pure woe
Until in a mood of blunt desperation
She asked him about their marriage relation

"You take me for granted," he said in reply.
"You need me so little." (She started to cry.)
"I need you, I want you, I love you," she said.
"Why didn't you say so? (His eyes were quite red.)
They wept there together repairing a rift
They both let it happen—they'd lost love's great gift.

Recapturing it, they began once again
To seek in each other love's sweetest refrain
The words were not spoken enough in the past
The silence, now broken, was filled at long last.
"I love you" was said in inspired ways new
"I need you" was noted and given its due.
To love one another is not quite enough
Without good expression the going gets tough.
If you love, make it known with your words and your
     deeds,
Fill with your presence your loved one's great needs.
"Beloved, you know that my love is for you."

FLIP

There is something
deliciously incongruous
about cleaning the basement
in my best dress;
serving hot dogs
to an honored guest;
Or wearing my blue jeans
to church.

It is almost
as daring
as letting my bare face hang out.

1970

Composite

I gave myself to me today
For close examination
I saw some superficial things
Which were not revelation.

With fear that I would find a blank
I pushed aside the trite
I made my way through vanity
I sought an inner site.

But when at last I found my core
And trembling, pulled aside its veil
I saw not me, but everyone
Who'd ever crossed my trail.

1974

CONFERENCE

A conference
In a world
Of men.
I stand
(Perhaps a bit
Uncertainly)
But on my own,
My earned
Place.
The question
Is inevitable,
Now and then.
Enough times
To be irritating.
"Are you
The wife
Of a delegate?"
Judiciously,
I bite my tongue
Suppressing
My instinct to
Answer sharply.
I murmur,
"I am a
Delegate."
How I would
Enjoy
Releasing
My put-down:
"No. Are you
The Husband
Of one?"   1974

CELEBRATION OF LIFE

I would compose a melody
To celebrate my life at Lent
My variegated chords and multipaced tempos
Will not be adequate
But they will be my thanks.

I would write a sonnet
To celebrate my life at Lent
My chosen words and clumsy phrasing
Will not be enough
But they will be my thanks.

I would perform a dance
To celebrate my life at Lent
My body will not be fluid and expressive
But it will show my thanks.

I would paint a picture
To celebrate my life at Lent
My inept lines and awkward design
Will not portray my joy
But they will be my thanks.

I would open to all my heart
To celebrate my life at Lent.
I may not succeed, but if I can
My God in Christ will know my thanks.

                                                    1974

*(Published in Cairns For Living, Washington Park
United Church of Christ, 1975.)*

OFFICE MOVE

Dust clouds are rising while furniture flies
People are fussing about office size.
"You move right there and I will move here,"
Who the hell must have his steno near?
Progress runs rampant and work is not done;
Salaries are paid for quick-shifting fun.
Everyone plays a ridiculous game
Of title and status, so what's in a name?
The nine to five workday excites me a lot;
The whole operation is going to pot!

1974

CONJUGATION OF LOVE

Lover,
You ask me to define love?
I am not at all sure
I can do this,
For I believe that
None of us knows
Love perfectly,
But only partially
And by degree
Each of us, though
Has experienced love
In one form or another
And we claim this pittance
As our right to say,
Mindless of the
Commitment involved,
"I love."

Let me be subjective

Love accepts me
For what I am;
It goes further to
Appreciate me for this.
Love sees what I can become;
It goes further to
Help me toward this vision.
Love asks nothing of me;
Expects a great deal,
But is not disappointed

When I fall short.
Instead, it offers me
Hope and Courage
When, whether I realize it
Or not, I need it the most.

This accepting love is there
At my blackest moments;
It is also present,
Rejoicing with me
When by some mischance,
Good fortune,
Or through my own effort,
I triumph.

Love accepts me
When I am most unlovable;
When I behave badly;
When I fail to
Consider those who
Depend on me;
When I am so self-oriented
That I not only do not
Function well,
But ignore the needs
Of others.

Love needs me, too
And it lets me know that need;
But when I cannot respond,
Love waits patiently and
Perhaps eternally
With me.

Love finds something in me
That is beautiful
And helps it to grow.
Love helps me to recognize
And obliterate
Those parts of me
Which are ugly.

Love disciplines me.
It helps me to
Accept my imperfections
While being aware of them.
It does not make me perfect,
But when love is present,
I strive to be better.

Love comforts me
When I am sad,
But it does not allow me
The luxury of self-pity.
Love diminishes my desire
For self-indulgence;
It mysteriously impels me
To offer my self
To others.
It does not permit
My self-glorification
Because it is so much larger
Than I.

Love is not innocent;
It is wise beyond belief.
It uses its wisdom
To keep me

From self-deception
And apathy. It will not
Let me hate; It will
Help me to understand.

It is exclusive to me
Because
Of my individuality;
It is inclusive
For all
Because
Of our commonality.
Love makes me
Aware of my life,
And finding it precious,
More aware of the preciousness
Of the life around me.

Love makes me love,
Not only in return,
But with an intensity
Which with ease
Is amplified many times over.

I have much to learn
About love;
Its nuances,
Its oneness,
Its wholeness.
If I take it a step
At a time,
Perhaps, maybe, someday,
I will live close enough
To love

To say with truth, humility,
And a measure of approval
From my Creator,
Not only
Am I loved,
But I love.

1974

Dance With Me

Dance with me!
The music begins.
Listen!
You can hear it too.

That slow beginning
Beckoning?
Those measured beats
And aimless, wandering melody
Tantalizing, nudging,
Searching for a soul
To enchant;
Building a pulsating
Pattern of harmony;
Weaving a net
Of tuneful charm;
Inviting abandonment.

Dance with me!
The music becomes
More enticing now;
Its insistent beat
Is too heady
To resist.

I am bewitched
And defenseless;
Immersed in sound
Helplessly captivated
By throbbing rhythm.
The piper plays

And I must dance;
The beat and the melody
Encircle me
With invitation.
My symphony and I
Must merge, must fuse
Grandly—into
A single, soaring entity
Of exuberant notes
And movement.

Dance with me!
Hear the music

Dance with me now,
For I cannot wait
Magnetized are
My mind and body

Dance with me!
Dance with me now!
I would not dance alone

But I must dance
Now.

Turn On

Hello.
I came
To turn you on.
I will not leave you
Until the appointed time
Has passed.
There is much about me
To desire.
But you must
Sharpen your senses
And hone your perception
Of me.
I offer you
A rich variety
Of experience
And unlimited growth.
I need very little
Feed me with joy
And water me with
Care and concern.
Burnish me with love,
And I will make you
Regent
Of my kingdom
Within you.
I will saturate
Your days and nights
With my presence;
Give an added fillip
To you worst
And your best times.

I am meant to be
Enjoyed; do so.
I am meant to be
Used; do so.
I am your agent;
Treat me well.
Do not restrain
Or inhibit me.
Do not reject me
Before you have
Given me full opportunity
To shine;
To show you
The hidden and the obvious
Magnificence
Of your world.
Hold me close
With an open hand.
Let me become
Your intimate
Companion.
Let me feed
Upon your being
That I may nourish others
Who, in turn,
Will nourish you.
I ask you only
For your love.
I would serve you well,
For I am Your Life.

GRATIFICATION

How lovely it is!
What delight
I take in it.
You gave me
The silly thing.

And I love it.

Were you telling me
Something
When you selected
Electric blue?
I revel in such
Artful flattery.
Its sensuous silkiness
Flows sheerly
From my shoulders.
I feel incredibly pampered
And adored.

I do not need it
To be a woman.

Because I am a woman
I will not part with it.

My first negligee.

Empathy

You cried for me
Because you cared;
I cried with you
Because you
Had shared.

REINFORCEMENT

Tell me that I'm lovely
Although it is not true
I'll know that you are lying
(That's just between us two).

Tell me that I'm charming
It sounds so good to me
No matter, dear, that it's not so
Someday, I hope to be.

Tell me that I'm sharp and keen
I'll lap it up like manna
It doesn't matter if I'm not
I'll still shout Joy-Hosanna!

But when you say you love me
Please leave the blarney out
Let me hear it straight and sure
I do not want that doubt.

TOGETHER-ME

Do not love me for my body
Praise not just my brain
Be not captured by my visage
Or my racial strain
Be not caught by my attention
Or my cooking skills
Do not deign to make a mention
Of my silly frills
Do not love me for my talking
Take a wider view
Find not intrigue in my walking
Know my bad side too
Love me not for one or two things
Leave no fact out
If your love can meet this standard
Love me without doubt.

You

You kiss me
And my desire
Quickens unconsciously
Yet I am deliciously aware
Of your body
And mine.
Because I love you.

You touch me
And my body responds
Rippling warmth
Permeates me.
I move closer
Because I love you.

You caress me
And fluid passion
Takes hold
I give myself
To you.
Because I love you.

You hold me
And I am mindless
Yet sensitized to
Your very pulse
Because I love you.

Our
Hungry consummation
Is limitless joy.
Because I love you.

ME

Your face, though always readable
Wears a public cover
I like it best when it's undressed
I know you then as lover.
Your body magnetizes mine
I move so I can face you
Sharpened senses feel you out
I reach out to embrace you
But I am not preoccupied
With savoring sensation
I see the fascinating crux
Of our intense relation.
I search your face so close to mine
For your unveiled abandon
The moment when your naked face
Reveals our hearts in tandem.
Your body I can hold and touch
In variegated fashion
But in your face I find your soul
—The target of my passion.

Modern Magdalene

Oh Lord I have a prayer for you
(I don't know how to pray!)
How can I love perfectly
When I get in the way?

I'm sure my love for You falls short
Of being what it could
When I, in passion, hold too tight
To that which I call good.

A single purpose love have I
But not for You, I fear.
Erotic, wild, but steady too,
For he whom I hold dear.

This kind of love is not enough
For him; he loves you more
Than I, who cannot understand
This man whom I adore.

I don't know how to love him
Although I care too much,
I think that I could find in You
The love I cannot touch.

And then, perhaps (Oh selfish me!)
I could express my care
For him (and then for others too);
I'd be a better me—I'd share!

More worthy of his love I'd be
I'm in the way—
I cannot pray—
Oh Lord.

LEAP OF FAITH

Too timidly
I stand
On the edge
Of potential
The mist of destiny
Obscures my vision;
Fills my lungs.
I cannot retreat.
I must tentatively skirt
My edge
Until
My hopeful leap
Reveals a
Mountain or
A deep abyss.

PROJECTION

Her mother's daughter
They say of you.
My lovely child,
How could this be?
You are all
I would have you be
And more.
But you are not me.
You reach in openness
For the world.
I approach it cautiously.
Your glowing zest
For life
I could not match.
Your healthy innocence
Was never mine.
Your sparkling beauty
Is not of your youth,
But of your spirit.
I rejoice in you,
Delight in your presence.
Perhaps it is because
You are you, or
Perhaps it is because
You are me
As I wish I had been.

Hell And Damnation

Being sure I'm right when the whole world says I'm am
    wrong;
Hearing the right music, but marching to the wrong
    song;
Failing to fulfill my potential and knowing it;
Knowing my best is not good enough and showing it—
                                 That's hell!

Being alone when I need companionship the most;
Having company when I would rather not play the
    host;
Receiving no love because mine is trapped inside me;
Needing a reason to love those who live beside me—
                                 That's hell!

Jealousy, which denies my own satiated need;
Envy which shows my own unwarranted selfish greed;
Resentment, which displays my own closed and empty
    hand;
Hate, which illuminates my failure to understand—
                                 That's hell!

The agony of suffering imagined torment;
The personality of that private intense ferment;
Knowing I cannot communicate my hell to you;
And worst of all, discovering my hell is quite true—
                          That's damnation!

Surgery

What kind of
Flagellation
Is this?
Compulsively,
I tear out
My guts—
To arrange them
Neatly
In tortured lines
On a piece of paper—
To inscribe them
Meticulously
With sharpened pen
And unshed tears.
I do not feel
The anguish of
Their removal
Until their
Revelation.

Dilemma

My hope abandoned
Would abolish
My fears.

But.

It would also
Condemn me
To the insensate
Inertia of
Death-life.

Vanity

Tell me I am getting fat
Get my answer plain and flat
      I've got
      No pot!
            That's that.

Secretly I'll start to fast
Sit-ups will be my repast
      I'll weigh
      Each day
            I've passed.

I'll shed pounds and lose inches
There'll be nothing left for pinches
      I'll win
      My thin
            San cinches.

When I've reached my final goal
I'll expect your ready dole
      Of praise
      To raise
            My soul.

I'll expect your proud attention
I'll anticipate your mention
      I'll hint
      My stint
            Abstention.

Will you notice how I look?
The work I've done, pains I took?
Oh woe
But no!
You schnook!

Revelation

Be me! you say,
And yet when I
Express my hidden self
You back away.
Are you repulsed
Or just afraid?

Tell you what
I think, you say,
So I unveil
For you. But
You're not there
To see me.

You want nothing.
Only my revelation.
I pull the curtain
And you turn away
Bemused.

Where is the balance?
How much of me
Is enough but
Not too little?
I too am disconcerted
By what is revealed.

Fraud

If all my world admires me
Why can't I still my fears
That I'm not as adequate
As most of my own peers?

Why can't I find the good in me
Which others seem to know
Although I search and probe within
Those virtues do not show

Yes, I reach out for people
Extend the helping hand
My reasons are obscure at best
Like salt in shifting sand.

I do not see the part of me
That others seem to savor
But surely there is something there
To give myself a flavor.

I love a lot, but know not why
And much of me I'll offer
But those who get are unaware
That more lies in my coffer.

Niggardly, I guess I am
Accepting adulation
Knowing well I've held some back
For undefined libation.

I know that I could give much more
And still not be bereft
Why do I stop so short of this?
There's always some that's left!

Why can't I give it all away?
(My cup will fill again)
Why do I live my life of sham
When there's so much to gain?

Why do I hold some back each time?
My guilt shouts loud and clear
You think you've got it all. I know
I'm fraudulent, my dear.

Wind-up

Springtime wind,
You blow today.
I step into you
With anticipation.
I face your fury;
Laughing.

You do not
Intimidate me.
Your blustering presence
Whips my clothes;
Disarranges my hair;
Fills my eyes
With fresh dust.

I walk into
Your challenge,
Exhilarated,
Receptive.
Your lashing strength
Cleanses me
And frees my soul
To soar
With you.

Discovery

I took a straight and narrow path
Because I heard 'twas right
With blinders on I made my way
Through every day and night.

My trip through life was easier
Because I chose that road
Its blandness and simplicity
Lightened up my load.

I did the normal usual things
Without much deviation
I did not see life's variance
I would not taste elation.

(Life's diversity is there
For those who see that choice
To reach and touch the spectrum whole
Is giving life a voice.)

So many times I wonder why
I lived my life half-through
Half-receptive, half-aware
With so much more to do.

I hurry now, I always have
I burst to make up time
I want each life experience
To mold myself sublime.

My soul, held captive many years
Is inexplicably free
Released from its protectorate
And bound no more by me.

I had caged it carefully
Afraid it would get lost
I did not know it's freedom
Would bring me gain, not cost.

My soul soars high and so do I
Through all of life's events
I absorb the good and bad
Eager and intense.

I know my reach is far too short
To gather all I seek
But now I do not fear to try
To reach life's highest peak.

Trap Door

My pencil whiles away my times
Of utter solitude
And sometimes when I'm busiest
I keep it close beside me
Sharpened and at hand
I never know which thought of mine
My pencil will command.
I write my inspirations down
As fast as they arrive
Some will die as they are writ
While others will survive.
My brain without a pencil stops
My tongue is incoherent
My romance with the written word
Is readily apparent.
I wonder as I write this theme
If pencils were abolished
Would my thoughts remain inside
Forever rough, unpolished?

STREET CHILD

Street child!
Yes, you—
With the wild black hair
And the dark eyes.
Mellifluous-deep
Sharp-shallow
Why won't you talk
With me?
Yes, you—
With the beginnings
Of womanhood
Etched more in your face
Than in your form.
Let me touch you.
Yes, you—
With the defiant-pathetic stance
And the wise ignorance,
The learned suspicion
Of a street child.
You swore at me once.
Yes, you—
In staccato Chicana,
Snapping, hating,
Pushing me away
With words
I did not comprehend.
You acknowledged me.
Street child!
Yes, you—
Who never weeps
—or laughs.

I want only to love you.
Why must I be content
To hold you only
With my eyes.

INDULGENCE

I beg your indulgence, I've heard you say
And were I not so craven,
I'd give you the lot of them, not, today
To keep in secret haven.

But how can I part with my sweet gluttony,
All my delightful pleasures?
I cling to them all as I cling to life
My vagaries are my treasures!

Of leisure I'm fond and for food I am wild
Drink? I will take a few glasses.
To dance is my joy, and parties my play
Men? I adore all their passes!

So beg of me not my indulgences;
They season life's savory stew
Please just look around for some for yourself
And leave me my own to rue!

Identity

Each day I walk
Through city slums
On my way
To my place
Of work.
The brown and crumbling
Buildings
Which I pass
Are half-deserted.
Old hotels house
The lonely old;
Behind greying
And cracked windows
They eke out their lives.

Where are those
Who love them?

Old woman!
You shuffle by me
Now and then.
Where are you going?
Have you something
To do?
Your clothes are
Shabby and shapeless.
You stockingless legs
Are blue-veined
And tired.
You dignity is weary, too
Though

Your ancient hat
Sports a plastic flower.
You do not smile.

Where are those
Who love you?

And you, old woman!
You are bizarre
Make-up-caked.
A clown parody
Of youth.
You have the
Same blue-veined legs
Displayed on
Spike-heeled shoes;
Revealed beneath your
Shortened skirt.
You smile
Enticingly grotesque
At stumbling broken men.

Where are those
Who love you?

Each day I walk
Through city slums
On my way
From my place
Of work.

I go home to
Those who love me.
I am not yet old.

Old woman!
Where are those
Who love you?

CONTENTMENT

My home is not a castle
It's small and not elite
It has no special features
It's really not too neat.

The color scheme is random
The furniture is worn
Any decorator would
Find it very forlorn.

Yet it has an aura that
Pervades each lived-in room
Something indefinable
Forbids all thought of gloom.

My home for me is comfort
A sensory retreat
I can safely be myself
In my favorite seat.

The door is always open
My friends pass through at will
No moat or gate forbids one
To come across the sill.

My home, while not a castle
Exudes its special air
Of love that's vast, accepting
Because you put it there.

RATIONALE

I could so easily retreat
Be none the worse for wear
I could function quite as well
Without your tender care.

Perhaps I'd get more reading done
Take time to scrub the floor
Partake of a love affair
Work a little more.

I might get a dog or cat
To keep me company
I'd listen to the radio
And sew exquisitely.

I'd write a book or sculpt a bit
Eat dinner with a friend
I'd fly to Florida in March
With lots of cash to spend.

Love, how I ramble on
You know this would not be
An empty shell can function well
It does not need the sea.

An empty life goes on the same
The body eats and drinks
But without you to feed my soul
My future, frankly, stinks.!

CHERISH ME

Cherish me
For I do not wish to leave you.
Show me your tenderness,
That I may respond in kind.
Give me your understanding
For I am only human.
Undergird me with your strength;
I am often tired.
Reveal your needs to me;
That I may fill them.
Hide not your weaknesses
I will match them with my own.
Love me overtly,
That I may love you fully.
And I will cherish you,
For I do not wish to leave you.

Defiance

I can stand tall alone
For I am strong enough
To deal with loneliness.

Pain does not touch me
For my psyche is scarred
And not susceptible.

I will carry your burden
But I will not let you
Put your shoulder to my load.

I would hold you close
But I cannot move into
The circle of your arms.

I am not strong.
I am fearful
And weak.

OUTER LIMITS

If you and I
Who are so close
Whose minds and hearts
Have met so often—

If you and I
Who share a life
Whose triumphs and sorrows
Are intermingled—

If you and I
Who have laughed and cried
Whose desires meet
In mutual release—

If you and I
Who need each other
Whose hopes and dreams
Mesh so neatly—

If you and I
Approach perfection
In our own relationship;
Come to total empathy—

Will we grasp
Love's total glory?

Or will we,
Stripped and barren,
Face destruction?

Warning!

I could love you
So easily.
Your gentle understanding
Pulls at my heart.
Your latent strength
Invites me
To its sheltering haven.

I could walk with you
In concert;
Talk with you
Without words;
Be with you
When I am not there.

I could love you
So completely.
I could absorb your love;
Meld it with mine;
And exclude the world.

I could love you
Recklessly,
Headless of consequence.

I
Could
Destroy you.
Please—be my friend.

NEED

The strength
Of your love
Entices me.

You would imbibe
My undiluted soul
In thirsty gulps.

You would purify
Its essence
To return it
In a sweeter portion
To me.

I am tempted
To quench your thirst.

INSTANT EMPATHY

My friend,
I have only met you
Today, But yet
I burst
With an impulse
To tell you
How much you mean
To me.
You smiled at me.
Brilliant, vulnerable.
Ready to relate to me.
I sensed your interest,
Your readiness
To count me
As friend.
I need you.
Have you a need
Which I can fill?
I do not have to
Explore you.
I know that you
Are my friend.
Let us sit together.

I Can't Wait

Patience is most virtuous
An art to cultivate;
Why is it so torturous
To bide my time and wait?

> (Outwardly I'm cool and calm
> Inwardly I ferment;
> I can feel not peaceful balm
> Patience is my torment)

I can't cooly wait for fate
To come to me at last
Each event goes its slow rate
Toward my full repast.

> (I hold my apprehension
> With hungry agony;
> My haste seems in suspension
> To those surrounding me.
> Little do they know that I
> Have reined my straining soul;
> My appearance shows that I
> Meander to my goal)

Though I burst through life to speed
I know this will not be
God has measured out my need
And life will pass through me.

Hindsight

Incarnate in my history
Are stages numbering to three
I would ask God for another
Patterned exclusively for me.

Childhood's stage was traditional
A necessary procession
From child to girl to womanhood
(And promptly into regression!)

There wasn't time to set the mold
My womanhood is not quite firm
I find a hundred thousand things
That I have yet to live and learn.

The second stage contained no time
To spend on my development
My time was never quite enough
For my own needs' envelopment.

I suppose I grew a little
The gift of myself to others
Stretched my skills and oiled my spirit
As it has for all wife-mothers.

Now suddenly, my place is first
Although my stage is numbered three
Some time is spent now on career
With lots available to me.

Yes I have time to grow some more
Time enough to spend on others
Time to do just as I would please
To execute all my druthers.

The fourth stage I would add is one
That I would with the others twine
To each phase of my lifetime span,
Awareness of this path of mine.

I would use each tiny time span
To think or pray or meditate
To rest or play or work a bit
And perhaps a better self create.

I would learn just who I am
How simple or complicated
I would know just why I am here
How, in God's plan, I am rated.

I would include a million things
In time consigned to careless waste
I would be a wider person
I would know how I am graced.

My life, a gift from God, goes on
My struggling soul lags far behind
Will the two meet 'fore life's end
Their ultimate purpose defined?

I dream—I ask too much of God
Upon His goodness I prevail
Sufficient is His gift of life
My choice is to succeed or fail.

Mourn Not

Life, whether
empty or full,
is as irreplaceable
as the moments
which mark its passing.

A full life
is not more precious
than an empty one.

But.
Perhaps.
It is easier to discard
than an empty one,
having, in each moment
of now,
been closer to
fulfilling its promise.

An empty life
cannot be relinquished
tomorrow
as freely,
for its potential
awaits exploration
and demonstration.

Experienced fully,
we must not weep
too long
at the demise

of great and noble figures
for their contribution
has been made
within the time
which God allotted
to them.
They have achieved
a measure of fulfillment.
Their indeterminate years
have been used well.

Let us weep, instead
for those lives
however long or short
which are marked
only by existence.
The tragedy of unawareness,
of apathy
of waste,
calls for more than tears.
It is cause for the
most extreme,
deepest-seated
unbearable grief.

God has given us talents
which can vary in number.
He has installed in us
a capacity for life
and the freedom
to exercise it.
He has also placed
an unknown time limit
on our earthy stay.

Those who grasp God's gifts eagerly,
and with joyful purpose
will expand yesterday,
inhale today, and exude.

Their lives
may not be pleasant always; indeed,
they may be sorrow-filled.
But each event is.

Do not weep for these.
Their awareness
has enhanced their lives;
and yours.

Shed your tears
for the unaware;
not only when their lives
have ended,
but while they merely exist,
oblivious to the treasure
they embody.

Never Done

I work for reasons manifold
Inherent in each view I hold
For money, yes, but more than that
Each job I do is where it's at
In tasks dull, or full of action
I find joy and satisfaction
Work I seek to chase despair
Love makes work because I care
Work I do to salve my heart
Toil I share to do my part
I have a hundred reasons more
To work with fervor at each chore
I know that without verve each task
Becomes too much of me to ask
But work approached with interest
Reveals a truth most manifest
Work performed with joy, I say
Becomes my most absorbing play.

CLOSE CALL

Death examined me
carelessly
today.
He scooped me up
in circumstance;
Turned me over and over
negligently
shrugged,
and cast me back
into life's garden
to ripen.

Wish

May my today
be a memorable
yesterday,
come tomorrow.

Status Unknown

My business life's an open book
My personal one's not hidden
I speak my mind unbidden.

There is but one area
Which frankly ain't your biz
Never, ever, ask me if
I'm Mrs., Miss or Ms.!

SHEHE

Be a man and do your thing;
Show your strength to me.
Be a bum or be a king;
But most of all, be *he*.

Maleness is your best domain;
Sacrifice it never.
Hold on tight to manly mien;
Keep your sex forever.

Remember, though your manhood
Is measured not by task
But by your very selfhood
And not a virile mask.

Allow that I am female;
Perceive my totalness.
Let your common sense prevail
To see my humanness.

I would not compete with you;
Nor you emasculate.
I would do just as you do;
I would not vacillate!

I would be most fully *she*
(It is my concrete right).
Dominate if right you be;
When wrong, see my insight.

Becoming is your manly being;
Obvious and complete.
I would like the selfsame sheen
My womanhood replete.

Let us both be all we can
Together and apart
I am woman, you are man
Fulfillment is our art.

MOVE OVER

I do not need your help, kind sir
I'll make it on my own
Just move your bod a little bit
That I may share your throne.

Make room for me at starting time
Right there beside you, please
I'll run the race to prove my place
Is not down on my knees.

Oh-ho! You feel uncomfortable?
Am I a threat to you?
Relax, old chap, I won't revolt
I merely want my due.

Your wisdom should reveal to you
Why joy you will attain
When I've my sights fixed on my rights
Your freedom you may claim!

Counter Weapon

How nice it is that woman is
Quite slighted by the law
(Except for passing reference
From the judicial maw.)

It leaves her free to do her thing
No doubts her brain must mull
Her lift can be exciting, filled
With challenge, not male-dull!

Work It Out

Hey, there, mister man!
I'm just as good as you
My brain works just as well as yours
A job like yours I'd do.

Now mind, I didn't tell you that
Our psyches matched exact
I know quite well the differences
And so do you, it's fact!

But I can do as much as you
In many situations
Better I would be, I'm sure
In certain operations.

I want my pay the same as yours
The self-same recognition
No special privilege, you hear?
I'd make that condition.

Why must I, so unlike you
Prove my talents twice
My rating should be just like yours
One standard should suffice.

Oh yes, I know we're different
I really am objective
You'll live your work and I'll like mine
The difference is—perspective!

(PAINT ME)

Paint me a picture of woman
Show her both tender and cruel
Embellish her head with brilliance
Give her the heart of a fool.

Color her warm getting warmer
Temper your strokes with some cool
Make her compliant and mellow
Add the strong will of a mule.

Sketch in the eyes of a temptress
Covered with purity's veil
Roughen her hands from a work load
Polish each long shapely nail.

Spray on a little indifference
Brush with some reckless concern
Portray her as somewhat selfish
Splatter with love to burn.

Dress here in furs and levis
Flesh her out soft and clean
Imply in her human weakness
Crown her a regal queen.

Artisan, why are you crying?
You can't do the job for me?
You don't understand today's woman?
Cheer up, friend, neither does she!

CHAINED

Confined upon my pedestal
I cried for my own lib
The crowd below me shouted when
They heard my message glib.

Secured, I could not see myself
As lofty, tall and free
Supported well, I could not tell
What matters most to me.

What if I fell from my high perch
Into the crowd below?
Would I be liberated
If so, how would I know?

Would I cast my eyes around
To search the crowd for you?
To find a million other me's
Which you could love as true?

Would I, too soon, begin to look
For freedom once again?
Would I, too late, long to return
To my most lofty plain?

(Turning back cannot be done;
I know this to be sound)
I stood; I cried; I fell; my pride
Took wing. Your love I found.

I hadn't known until that time
That it was always there
That I was only chained by me;
That I am free—you care!

Sexsolution

They have a problem to work out
There is not time for facts
Each must overcome some doubt
While information lacks.

He is snookered, in a crunch
For finding a solution
All he has is a simple hunch
From his male evolution.

She can really get to it
Because her female gender
Leaves her free to intuit
Decisions she can render!

EXPLORATION

I hide today.
My enigmatic shell
Will not betray me.
My soul has gone
Exploring;
The door to my heart
Is locked.

I am lost inside
But strangely home.
I see with
Different vision
My familiar secrets.
I do not recognize them.

I hear you
Faintly calling me
But I am absorbed
In my multilevel maze
Of contemplation
—and confusion.

I am not me today.
I am no one.
I cannot answer you.

I am busy
Collecting my
Scattered parts,
Puzzling
Over their fit;

Piecing and repiecing
That I may become
Wholly me.

Do not knock.
I am hiding inside.

Moving Up

Now that I have a window for plants
And a sunshiny office in which to dance
Delusions of my grandeur pop into my mind
I'm lacking a few things I simply must find.

The color of carpet's not pleasing to me
A nice hearty rust would be nicer to see
The drapes, I'm afraid, will not do at all
I'd like a leaf print, suggestive of Fall.

The walls, not offensive, had better be done
In paper exclusive, they'd be much more fun
Some pictures to hand, original, natch—
Would jazz the decor, but they'd better match!

And just for a final touch, understand,
Because water and coffee are simply too bland
A bar and its fittings would make each day great
With ☑ all of the above I will operate!

MASK

Where is my mask?
I have searched
Everywhere;
It is gone.
My raw and tender being
Suffers.
I am scorched
By
Passion;
Withered
By despair;
Frozen by my lack
Of understanding
I bleed
From useless exposure.
I seek strength;
It is not revealed.
I would welcome numbness;
It does not appear.
Where is my mask?
I remember now.
I tore it off
And cast it away forever
For a moment of joy.

The Giver

I would fill your needs
But I cannot see them.
Open your isolation to me.

I would share my love with you
But I cannot empty my heart.
Replace my outpouring with yours.

I would add myself to you
But I cannot find the space.
Make room in yourself for me.

I would give my soul to you
But I need yours in return.
Merge your separateness with mine.

I would be
Individual, yet composite
Emptying and filling
Part of you and all of me.

You are alone
And I need you.

THE RECEIVER

Do not extend your gift to me
Unless it is wrapped in yourself
Your gifts alone are meaningless;
Without your love for me
Your gift is but a gesture.

Only your love can see my need;
Only your love can fill it.

Do not show me your heart;
Let me in!
Do not lay bare to me your soul;
Pull me into it!
Do not understand me;
Step into my being.

And when our hearts and souls
Have commingled,
Our twoness will be
One together and ten apart.

Your gift will have enriched the world;
It will have begun
A perpetuity of love,
Overflowing, immersing and suffusing
Others in empathy;
Destroying the curse
Of loneliness.

CONFIDANT

Why are you
Afraid of me?
I have no deadly weapons.
I would not
Harm you.
I would have you
Free, unchained and whole;
Strong enough
To accept
The exposure of
My secret being.
I seek only
A receptacle
For the thoughts
I cannot contain
Within me.
I would
Entrust to you
The seething spillover
Of my soul
For safekeeping.

MARTYRDOM

I save my moods from day to day
The hurts and slights I've taken
Imagination has its way
I feel alone, forsaken.

But life and I continue while
I make no public sigh
Six days weekly I can smile
Thursday is my day to cry.

INSECURITY

You said "I have always
loved you."
And I began
To live again.

Split!

Your unconscious
Shuts me out.
Imperceptibly.
And yet I know.
I cannot open
Your inner door
Because you say
It is not locked.
My frustration
Shuts you out.
Blatantly!
My despair
Accepts the blame
For our
Fractured relationship.

INSIDE TRACK

Just because he's nice to you
Doesn't mean you should
Assume he loves you madly
Though I'm sure you wish he would.

Just because he cares for you
Doesn't mean he's yours
I think you'd better realize
His heart has many cores.

He has concerns for children
Some for many friends
Some for those who need him most
His love list never ends.

He has some special places
For the old and for the poor
His heart holds many faces
As beloved, to be sure.

He cares a lot for everyone
And for a special few
He gives much more than asked of him
(Which others seldom do).

But please, my dear, make no mistake
Although he holds you high
His love for you is not the kind
For which you seem to try.

That very special part of him
To which you have no key
Is not for you at all because
It's occupied—by me!

Spit It Out!

Friend, don't play it coy with me!
I know what you are after.
Silly games are not my thing
(I can't suppress my laughter!)
Gallantry is not your style
Romantic words aren't mine;
Forget about that dinner out
And scrap your jug of wine.
I can see you've always tried
To ask a girl correctly;
Can't you give it to me straight?
I'll answer you directly!

COVERUP

I don't care if he loves another
I don't care at all
I have things to do, you know
I can't wait for his call.

I don't care if he bares his soul
Why should it bother me?
Let him play with other fems
Alone I'd like to be.

I don't care if he shares his love
With all the world around
I don't care if I get the scraps
Who needs it by the pound?

I don't care if he's home or not
It gives me time to cry
I don't care, no I really don't
If I live or if I die.

Forced Wisdom

I do know how
To hold you.
But I am a woman;
Torn, distressed;
Of contradictory parts.
My love for you
Is not crafty enough
To keep you constantly
Beside me.

My all-consuming
Possessiveness
Makes barely tolerable
The opening of my hands
To release you.
My naked heart
Pours forth
Unspoken longing
For you (Stay!)
While with forced wisdom
My lips say "Go!"
I will wait.

I avert my eyes
For they are
Uncontrollably stripped
Of pretense
I know they would haunt you.
Go!

Do not pacify me
With your presence.
I will know your
Restlessness.
I let you go reluctantly.
I want everything
Of you; you owe me
Nothing.
My selfishness is
Insatiable;
Impossibly demanding.
I do not speak of it.
Do not see my agony.

I will wait
Until my clamoring heart
Has quieted.
I will deal with
My temporary loneliness.
You will return
To erase it
Because I have not
Asked you to say.

Cool It

I'll tidy up my feelings
And put them in a drawer
And when the time comes some day soon
I'll take them out once more.

Meantime, I will try to grow
More strong and less intense
Outwardly I'll care much less
(It's but a fool's pretense).

My love for you is of a sort
That could be quite destructive
And so I'll back away from you
And seek advice instructive.

Oh, I will learn—I'll try most hard
To temper my emotion
To reason with my passion and
Apply love's cooling lotion.

I'll love you but I'll hold you not
My lips will not demand you
Warm and tender I will be
Not once will I command you.

I'll hold you not but still I'll pray
That you'll keep coming back
I'll prune my anger, slave my hurt;
I will not, must not crack!

And someday soon I'll open wide
That pain-filled drawer marked "thine."
To find its contents not the same
God's will be done, not mine.

Jetrip

We hang suspended
Over the giant roulette wheel
Of the earth.
God gives it
A handy spin
And after a careful examination
Of the options
We settle comfortably
Into our selected slot.
We wait in the heavens while
God moves the earth
For us.

1975

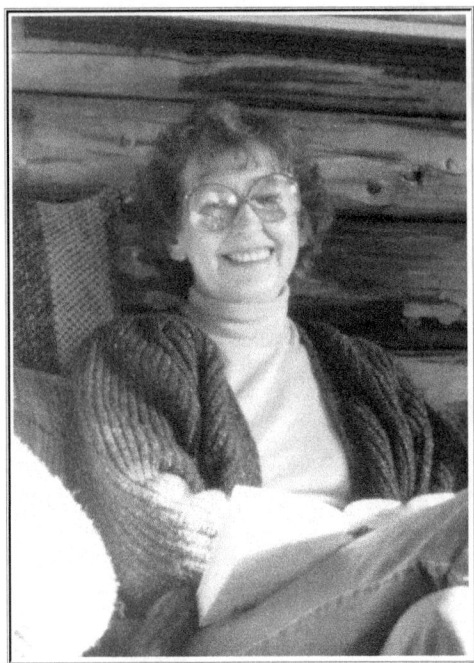

Does It Matter?

I have stopped asking the question "Who am I?" because
     I know that the answer is unimportant.
Nor do I worry about who I was,
Or who I will be. I am not the same person I was yes-
     terday, nor will I be the same come tomorrow.

The question of why I am here no longer causes me
     puzzlement.
The "why" doesn't alter the fact that I am here.
Whether or not my life has a purpose is a question that
     is paled by the first two, already meaningless.

I accept the indisputable fact that—at least within my
     personal perception, **I am**. Too, I accept the fact that
     I am **here**. My purpose, if indeed I have one, is
     known only to God, who created me and placed me
     here after gifting me with a free will, an abundance
     of intelligence, and a superfluity of sensitivity. But I
     am confined by my here-ness and limited by my
     now-ness.

I am, I am here. I am here now. The least—and perhaps
     the most—I can do is think and feel and love and do
     and grow. My identity and my direction will evolve
     unperceived by me; if they are to have significance,
     it will not matter much, for that significance can
     only be a fleeting moment in eternity.

It is enough.

                                                    1975

THE PRICE

You said it; Loving is not enough.
And of course, you are right.
But why, when I ask more of you, do you say:
I love you. What more could you want?
And I am ashamed.

You said it: My love is inclusive, not exclusive.
And that is good.
But why, when I examine our commitment, do I feel
    cheated?
Am I not blessed?
I feel only despair.

You said it: I am a giver, demanding nothing.
And that is selfless.
But why are my gifts valueless to you?
You accept nothing.
And I am nothing.

You said it: My love is great enough for all.
And that is Christ-like.
But why do I feel anonymous, lost in the crowd;
Reaching, but unseen; screaming unheard for sharing?
Aghast at my debasement.

You said it: Loving is not enough.
And you are right.
Because the price of your love is too high.

Why do I pay it so willingly?

                                        1975

A Matter Of Life—

I want, I want, I want—
I don't know what I want
But something in me
Wants
With relentless ferocity
Pushing and nagging from within
Tinging my joy
Ridiculing my sorrow
Refusing me peace in repose
Veiling and obscuring
The simply beauty
Of the dailiness of life.
I yearn for explosive tranquility
And calm furor
Unwarranted ecstasy and
Unearned despair.
I would wrap a lifetime
Of sensuality and
An eternity of knowledge
Into the divine and damning
Moment of now,
Leaving nothing unexplored
But death.
But I do not want to die.

                                          1975

VACATION

Suffer, all ye hapless souls,
You have to work this week!
Dross ain't here to make your day
Please contain your pique!

Monday she'll be back with you
To plague you once again
Control yourselves and carry on
You can wait till then.

TELEPHONE OPERATOR

I plugged him in
For the fortieth time today
And he wants me
To make *another* call
For him!
Me—with a switchboard
Lit up like a Christmas tree!
So I let him wait.
Well, of course he got mad
And hung up.
Then he had the *nerve*
To come storming
Out of his office
To let me know
That he was *important*.
"I'm a busy man,"
He said. "I can't
Wait all day
While you sit around
Filing your nails."
"Mister," I said,
Why don't you go
Back to your office
And do you yours?"
(There's nuthin' wrong
With his dialing finger.)
Della, the new relief gal
—She's had trouble
With him, too.
Boy, he really
Read her off

A couple of times.
And she's a *good* worker
Learnin' fast.
I feel kinda protective
Toward her.
So I tell her,
"Just mind your P's and Q's,
Honey, and don't let him
Give you no flak."
So what he's worth a
Few million.
He ain't no better'n
You and I.
He's just another man.

School Finance

Educating people is a fact of life, we know;
But funding it is something else—where *does* the money
    go?
For special ed or transportation, books and building,
    too;
Reading, writing, 'rithmetic, and history old and new;
For teachers, driver, janitors, and office help galore.
How can we ever list it all—there's more and more and
    more!
But worse than how the money's spent is "who should
    pay the bill?"
Federal, state, and local funds parade right through the
    mill.
But in the last analysis (this goes from bad to worse);
The individual citizen must empty out his purse!

UNMANNED

An unmanned office is a thing of beauty
The girls hang in there to do their duty
A female lawyer answers the phone
A project director is a typing drone
A research assistant can point out the biffy
Librarians can register men in a jiffy
Females must work regardless of rating
The male needs his time for operating!

MY FRIEND

Because you are my friend
You offer me your mind
To explore; to meet at every corner
My thoughts twin kin to yours.

Because you are my friend
You offer me your heart
As sanctuary; to find in it
My own intensity subtly matched.

Because you are my friend
You offer me your cup
To drain; but I cannot
I must, in joyful agony, fill it up.

1976

Is Anyone Listening

If you would please me,
Know that I am woman
Completely human
Touched with divinity
Mired in imperfection
Defined not by what I do
But by what I am.

Woman!
No less than man
And no more.

Intellect, softened by intuition
Calculation, subverted by passion
Desire, controlled by ambition
Pettiness, opposed by magnanimity
Impetus, cut short by pragmatism
Bitterness, made palatable by love.

  Hold me!
  If not in your arms
  —within your heart

  Touch me!
  If not with your body
  —with your soul

  Caress me!
  If not with your hands
  —with your spirit

Speak to me!
If not with your tongue
—with your mind

It is too late, too late
And I must settle
For your awareness
That I am woman.

1976

WHAT IF IT WORKS?

What if it works?
Say that I win
Top out the effort
End the begin?
Where will I go then?
What will I do?
Once at the apex
Am I not through?
Champions are lonely
They stand high away
Their feats set up fences
That keep love away.
What if I make it?
Why should I try?
Losers keep living
And winners just die ....

                                                    1976

Spilled

I have more to present
Than you are ready to take
But I cannot carry my offering
Alone, or for long.
Like a water mill,
I scoop my elusive gifts
From a rushing mystic brook
To raise them exultantly high
In momentary tribute.
You are not quick enough
Nor is my strength sustained
And my unappraised burdens
Spill heavily away.

1976

HANDS

Hands that speak the most to me
Are broad and strong, exciting, free
Hands that move with studied ease
Control an eagerness to please
Hands that promise warmth and fire
Spark the touchstone of desire
Hands I want to stroke and hold
Are sensitive and not quite bold
Hands that tempt my very soul
Are destined for another role ....

1976

TICKLE ME

Yes, it pleasures me to tease you
But sir, your controlled response
Belies your understanding
Of my flippant invitation—
My lightly phrased intent.

So you would like to tickle me?
But sir, your touch is much
Too casual to be accidental
Too infrequent to be unplanned
Too nebulous to be meaningless.

Tickle me at will, but know
I will not be moved to laughter,
Nor will you. The tide of our attraction
Will putt us not toward levity;
It will submerge us both in ecstasy.

A Hundred Years Ago

I looked at you
A hundred years ago
I saw a man—no more.
I made a cool appraisal
And saw a man—no more.

I felt your gaze
A hundred years ago
I sensed your warmth—no more.
I made a cautious judgment
And sensed your warmth—no more.

I heard you speak
A hundred years ago
I heard a man of wisdom
I made a short analysis
And heard a man of wisdom.

I spoke to you
A hundred years ago
I knew you heard my soul
I made a wary circle,
And knew you heard my soul.

You told me that you cared
A hundred years ago
I heard your hint of love
I made an unbelieving check
And heard your hint of love.

I told you of my love
A hundred years ago
I felt your heart enfold me
I made a hesitant retreat
And felt your heart enfold me.

You and I first met
A hundred years ago
Today we hold our interlude
Cupped in secret hands
Today we hold our interlude.

You and I cannot complete
Our unplanned empathy
We can but savor our intent
Unsought, but recognized
A hundred years ago.

1976

ONE TO ONE

You and I travel
Together for now.
Our touching and sharing
Are glorified by oneness,
But there is a twoness
About us—
That is indisputable.
My experience cannot be yours
Titillate me.
You cannot choose my path
For me;
Nor is it possible for me
To lure you from your vision.
The immediacy of your reality
And mine
Separates us,
As our awareness of these realities
Unites us.
(Our perceptions are not equal.)
As we are together
You and I are alone
Exploring mutually
Exclusive territories
(Virginal, tempting;
Ancient, threatening)
Mine—unknown by you;
Yours—obscure to me.
Though we cling tightly
To each other,

Reveling in our rapport,
Our unique realities
Will never merge.

1976

Never Goodbye

We never said goodbye.
You didn't want to.
So when you left, you were still here.
Not present, but not absent either.
The conversation we began
Was never ended.
There was a long hiatus,
Mid–sentence;
But no lack of communication.
Why should I say "hello"
I'll just speak my continuing thoughts
Out loud.
For the exercise, of course,
Because you know them in advance.
Good friend, your priceless gift
Of warm rapport
Is part of me.

                                                    1976

Doggerel

Warren, dear Warren, now please let me check
How does it feel to be the exec?
Will it go to your head?
Or will it instead
Make you a big nervous wreck?

Warren, dear Warren, I really must know
How you intend to get on with the show
Will you do it remote?
Or let us all vote?
Can you make this bureaucracy go?

Warren, dear Warren, I know you'll excel
Our image will prosper with you "on the sell"
I see you stand tall
So here is the ball
Just grab it—and scramble like hell!

1976

Plunge

I watched you strip yourself
Quite close to bare
The other day.
I felt with you
Your twinge of uncertainty
Before your resolute plunge
Into humble vulnerability.
Your humanness, exposed,
Quivered a bit
Underneath a confident exterior;
Perhaps expecting
An onslaught of denial
—or rejection.

You did not quite believe
That what I knew
Would prove true for you.
Was it bravado, or courage,
In response to my challenge?
I hope it was your faith
In my assurances,
But it does not matter.
You stripped yourself,
Putting your naked psyche,
Defenseless, on the line
For critical examination.

You passed, you know.
You laid bare your human failing
And they revealed themselves
As manifestations of great strength.

Your credibility instantly tripled.
Your faith has been sustained.
And unanticipated love
Now reaches out to
Encompass you.

1976

(Leg Review)

The number of issues of Leg Review
Which we facetiously call it
Has to be cut quite a bit for the current year
And God, we don't mean to maul it!

But yes, on occasion our quality slips
But our fervor affirms dedication
Our priceless words have their firm intent
But they cry for interpretation.

Please understand our artistic mode
It's poetry for decision
It's not that we want to be wrong at all
But we're tainted with imprecision!

If now and then we are not quite clear
In the pace of our haste we get spaced!
We know that our readers will snicker and howl
With our follies we always get faced.

Thank you for writing just the same
It was a delightful letter
If that's what we get when we goof just a bit
Next time, we'll try to do better!

(Sometime)

I needed someone's time
Some sunlight and some love
I looked almost unceasingly
For someone's beckoning nod
To lure me far away
From clock-bound duties
—and numbness.

Someone had to understand
My blind denial
My plodding habit-stance;
My cursed duty-bound obsession.
I needed someone's hand
To pull me from my work and
Into glory.

I needed someone's will
To teach me how to play;
To peel from me my hard veneer
Of practicality.
I needed someone's warmth
To thaw my frozen spirit.
I needed someone's words
To help me fly.

You gave to me an afternoon,
When I needed you.

1977

SHARE

Share with me, you cry
    And so with me, cry I
    See me in my life, I plead
Your life, not mine, say you
    Speak of your concern, I add
My thought, not yours, sigh you
    Come with me, I ask
Your trip, not mine, dodge you
    Believe with me, you shout
I am not you, sob I

We understand we stand   alone.
We reach in vain across   an intimate abyss.
And like   familiar strangers.
We try to   love.

1976

SEPTEMBER'S ASPEN

September's aspen
Lit your face
with golden urgency

September's breezes
teased your hair
with impish ecstasy

September's sunshine
warmed our love
beyond anticipation

September's glory
found my hands
And I became September.

                                                                    1977

From A Controlled Lover

Each time I leave you,
I curse myself;
Ruefully aware
That I have walked away,
not having reached for you.
When we are together,
my mind, in sweet communion with yours,
sends forth my unspoken
expression of love.
And while I hope
that you will know my muted thoughts,
and understand,
I am afraid that you will.
Our carefree conversations
are marred by my longing
to hold between my hands, your face.
The flippant quips
that pass so smoothly from my lips
divert them from the magnet of your mouth.
I suspect you know
that the crinkled merriment
in the eyes unwillingly veils
my stifled desire.
I clasp your hand,
knowing that I must not hold you;
fiercely wanting your caress,
and retreating from my need to accept it.
The tenuous balance
of our divided oneness
is set on history's blind and unperceptive scale.
I dare not move, except away,

lest I stumble into confusion and despair
the innocent, trusting and cherished ones
who share and enrich our lives.

Damn society!
What I want I cannot have;
what I have I cannot want!
I dream of potential fulfillment;
sensing all too strongly
that my dream come true
would be an unforgivable nightmare.

Perhaps it is I who should be damned.

1977

HANDLE WITH CARE

Love me gently, please
Loosen my reins with care
Oh, I know
Our rendezvous is long delayed.
So long, too long
We have obeyed
Reluctantly strong controls
They are tight;
Invisible bonds
Of self-inflicted restraint
Ambiguous protection
For you—and for me.

Love me slowly, please
Move me at a measured pace
Oh, I know
Your touch invited immersion.
So long, too long
We have deferred our eager plunge.
My want is fierce
As yours; sublimate
But too strong to quell
I am afraid
For you—and for me.

Love me fully, please
This change may be our last
Oh, I know
That life goes on
So long, too long
When you are gone.

We have stayed our souls
Until my September.
Hold me for a timeless moment
Lest I explode before
Our joy is quite complete.

Love me—love me—love me
It is late, so very late
Oh, I know
You would leave me
With your memory replete
So long, too long
I have waited
For life's rationale.
And now I know,
Almost too late—
It is you.

1977

PRAYER FOR REMEMBRANCE

I need to remember

My past, for it is a blurry marathon
of selfishness and greed
of thoughtless ignorance
and superficial concern.
I have indulged myself
with careless irritation
and unforgivable apathy.

I have withheld my gifts
when they were needed;
only to offer them
where they were unwanted.

I have loved deeply,
but without communicating my love.
I have known agonizing care,
but have not been moved
to its active expression.

But I have learned as well
that I am not alone
in my timid thoughtlessness.
Like others, I have felt
unjustly used, perhaps
as I have dealt with them.

I have cried out silently
for an expression of care from others.
When I have not received,

I have been hurt and angry,
failing to understand
While I nursed and reveled
in my pain.

When the care of others
has been lavished undeservedly on me
I have been touched, grateful
and puzzled, for my capacity for love
has been nurtured toward growth.

As I have been reached,
so would I reach.
As I have been loved,
so would I love.

I need to remember
because I need to care
over and over and over again.

1977

Here And/or There

—While you're not here
Talk to me
    Sing to me
        Hum in my ear

Read to me
    Bring to me
        Thoughts I would hear

Think with me
    Dream with me
        And I'll add my share

—While I'm not there

                    1977

WHY CRY?

The little child may wonder why
the old so often softly peer at life
Through brimming, tear-filled eyes.
"Why do they cry, no matter what?"
Why indeed?
Innocence does not cry; it laughs
when moved by joy.
Tears are brought forth stormily
by skinned knees and spankings.
Grownups do not cry.
"What need is there?"
Joy can still be celebrated with laughter
or hugged inside and saved.
Skinned knees and spankings are replaced
by secret sorrows best unshared,
uncomprehended, unridicled.
Feeling tears are stored unshed
in memory's capacious casks;
left to mature into the bittersweet wine
of aged sentimentality.
No time to cry, no time; no place—
only stifled reasons.
The little child is born
with storage places for tears,
but does not use them.
"Why should tears be saved?"
Why, indeed?
The answer come at the edge of age
When the brimming cask of harbored tears
spills over ...

And one discovers that
There is no need to hoard.

1977

To My Unnecessary Friend

I must not
seek your company too often,
lest our irreplaceable rapport
be dulled by repetition.
We must not
fill each other's needs too completely,
lest they lose their teaching edge.
Let us struggle in mutual awareness
but on our own.
Your attunement strengthens me
and affirms my being,
but I must not be denied
my triumphant victories
or my dreadful defeats.

Be my unnecessary friend;
my bonus confidant;
my special companion—
the surprise ingredient
in my cherished cup of joy,
that my random sips will be
sweetened exquisitely.
Oh, be my constant friend forever,
but not to satiation
for I must orchestrate for me
and you must sing your song.
All that we can truly share
is a perfected measure
of added grace and harmony.

1977

No More

I left you;
taking only a few
memory-laden pieces;
wanting nothing more—
no more! no more!

I left you;
dazed by my own arrogance
dream-walking into
the unknown, wanting
no more! no more!

I left you;
keeping company
with your self-made vision
of me, wanting
no more! no more!

I left you;
shedding my plastic image
empty beyond years,
bereft, but wanting
no more! no more!

I left you;
defeated by our past,
indifferent to my now,
numbed, and wanting
no more! no more!

I left you;
in my place you hung
a life-size girlie nude.
Oh, God! Was there
no more! no more!

I left you;
while I held the top
of a cleansing sigh;
peace-bound, and wanting
no more! no more!

1978

*(Published in American Poetry Anthology, Vol. 1,
No. 3-4, John Frost, Editor, 1982.)*

THE MIDDLE OF THE BED

Ah.
The luxury,
and the loneliness,
of sleeping in the middle of the bed.
At first,
spread-eagled, exploring, reaching;
then prone,
inquiring into the mattress for human
warmth.
A restless tossing, side to side,
before a final settlement
for a half-accepted haven
of rumpled bed clothes
enfolding my curled-up form.
Sleep comes slow,
and deep inside,
a resentful passion stretches out its
mindlessness,
seeking arousal that is not there.
My swelling need
pushes at my outside walls
until they ache
into the silence of solitude;
remembering, seeking, quivering, eager for
the caring touch
of human hands.
Be still, desire!
Retreat!
You search an empty love,
not here, not ever.

Ah!
Hold me, someone;
in the luxury of my loneliness,
courting sleep
in the middle of the bed.

1978

(TO DANCE)

Long ago, I invited you
to dance with me.
The prelude has been
unnecessarily long.
I was ready too soon;
and able too late.
I thought it would be
easy. My self-made
chains would melt away
and I would lift my feet
and raise my arms
and dance, dance, dance!
An unrealistic yearning,
that. I did not know
that chains, thickened
and hardened by habit,
must be hacked and chopped
away. I did not know
that flesh and soul would
emerge mutilated, brutalized.
Give a moment to heal
I still want to dance!

1978

(Free)

Well.
Look at me.
My soul has been exhumed.
My life is mine,
not yours.
The sureness of strain;
my comfortable harness;
my silken, airless cocoon
I've slashed and left behind.
A wrenching escape to
Awesome freedom
from your domain.
I offered you my soul
—a foolish move,
but not more mad
than yours.
You *took*
my bounty casually,
wrapped it unprotesting
inside your smothering need
and put it away.
Late, late I know
that I must soar
and wheel and BE
untramelled, unrestrained.
My treasured, willful being
chooses me as home;
my boundaries are mine!

Oh, God, I'm free!
I'm almost me—

—a novice,
learning anew
how to live.

1978

(Harvest)

The dim dog days of summer
hold me indolently
in my sweaty lethargy;
caring not,
feeling hot,
alone with no one.

Spring's been, you know;
her breath-freshened mornings
wrapped me greenly
in lassitude,
for solitude,
alone with me.

Can winter come
when fall's not begun?
Surely autumn's busy afternoon
will design me,
define me,
for someone's alone.

Winter, stay your heavy chill
I ripen late this life
It's harvest time and I'm still new!
Diminished? Some.
But finished? Un—
Pluck me after my alone
is someone's.

1978

Baby Doll

Poor baby doll, you're not quite right;
a fix or two will do it,
a pat, a pull, a push or three
(Might help a lot to true it.)

I'll just adjust your arms and legs;
and straighten out your head.
The styling of your hair's all wrong
(It's flat and looks quite dead.)

Your talker either runs too fast
or will not work at all.
Of course, you're fine the way you are
(My not-quite-perfect doll.)

But, dear, my work is never done
You still need some correction.
I'll leave you on the shelf a while
(You still have my affection.)

I'll dust you now and then because
You're handy when I need you.
I'll play with you when fancy strikes
(Occasionally, I'll feed you.)

Forgive me if you tumble town
and crack your head wide open.
Remember, I can fix it all
(Even spilled emotion!)

Trust in me, you'll soon be whole
I'll just ignore your crying
Fixing sometimes pains a bit
(But gosh, you can't be dying!)

Flowers for your sightless eyes;
My magic always works!
A plaintive tune for deafened ears;
What's this? A heart? It hurts!

1978

Yo Yo

I will and I won't
I do and I don't
I cannot understand me.
I'm sure and I'm not
I'm cold and I'm hot
How can I even stand me?

I waver, then hold
I'm timid, then bold
I wallow in indecision.
I can, then I can't
I laugh, then I rant
My thoughts have no precision.

I'm clear as a bell
Then muddy as hell
Whatever could be the matter?
I'm glad and I'm sad
I'm good and I'm bad
Plainly, I'm mad as a hatter.

But just when I think
I'll jump in the drink
Belatedly I will remember
That I'm not unique
In my ease then my pique
The human race counts me a member.

Time Out For Me

Leave me alone and let me be
Like me the way I am
I'm too old to need your guiding hand
And too young to need a keeper

I'm living my life the way I choose
Your details don't amuse me
I'm finding my plan in a grander scan
My reason for being is deeper

If I forget to turn off the light
Space out a meal or two
Remember too late that I have a date
I'm *not* face-to-face with the reaper

I'm living my life the way I choose
My family tasks are done
I'm holding a job and paying my way
While becoming a right-brained leaper

Talk with me, sit with me. Come we'll have
fun
I'm finding my richness and joy
My living scheme is a lifelong dream
Why should I settle for cheaper?

4/5/1984

(Christmas)

Christmas is coming!
I see it
    —in the rose and silver dawn of spring
    —in the fierceness of summer sun
    —through the glitter of an aspen-laced fall
    —in the harshness of a winter glare.

Christmas is coming!
I see it
    —in the steady flow of mellow candles
    —in the neon reality of a big city
    —on a lamp-lit, softened country road
    —in the elegant tongue of a hearth-made fire

Christmas is coming!
I see it
    —reflected in your eager eye
    —gleaming from a stained-glass window
    —bouncing off a shiny moon
    —warming up a darkened room.

Christmas is coming!
I see it
    —a world of light come close
    —the brilliance of an evening star
    —shouts to all that Christ is here
    —and I turn on—inside.

1978

Finished

I've closed your path into my life,
I said goodbye, remember?
I've tidied up the trail you left,
And doused each smoking ember.
Covered over all your signs,
Allowed the weeds to flourish,
Moved myself to unknown ground,
Stemmed my need to nourish.
Found new friends and things to do,
Buried passion deep inside,
Turned myself away from that,
Found highways free and wide.
Cropped my hair and changed my look
Given up romance …
How could you call? We're through, you
know,
Well—maybe one last dance ….

7/21/1982

Epilogue

Doris died quietly at home on August 3, 1986, eight months after she was diagnosed with malignant brain cancer. Other than to have children, this was her only experience of being hospitalized. Thanks to the Hospice program she died with her dignity intact.

Doris was a strong introvert, she always kept part of herself to herself. During her last months she chose to reveal that inner self, and we—her family and friends—came to know and appreciate another side of her. To the end, through pain and severe medication she was able to maintain her sense of humor, her honesty, and her clarity of thought. Her thinking life was always of utmost importance to her.

May your memories of Doris bring you joy and edification. She would like that.

Phillip A. Ross